ALEC JENSEN

HACKING

Unveiling the Secrets of
Cybersecurity and Ethical Hacking
(2024 Guide for Beginners)

Copyright © 2024 by Alec Jensen

All rights reserved. No part of this publication may be reproduced, stored or transmitted in any form or by any means, electronic, mechanical, photocopying, recording, scanning, or otherwise without written permission from the publisher. It is illegal to copy this book, post it to a website, or distribute it by any other means without permission.

Alec Jensen asserts the moral right to be identified as the author of this work.

First edition

This book was professionally typeset on Reedsy. Find out more at reedsy.com

Contents

1	Introduction	1
2	Introduction to Hacking	3
3	Ethical Hacking vs. Criminal Hacking	11
4	Passive and Active Attacks	17
5	Mapping Out Your Hacks	21
6	Basic Spoofing and Man in the Middle Attack Techniques	29
7	Hacking Passwords	36
8	Hacking a Network Connection	39
9	Popular Tools for Hacking	45
10	How to Hack a Website	49
11	Conclusion	53

1

Introduction

Engaging in hacking represents a fascinating skill that demands a deep comprehension of computer functioning. While society often associates hackers with criminal activities, involving the unauthorized acquisition and unethical use of information, it is essential to recognize the multifaceted nature of this practice. Beyond the negative connotations, there exists a community of ethical hackers who acquire these skills with the sole intention of safeguarding themselves, their families, or the businesses they are affiliated with. Additionally, there are individuals who explore unauthorized systems out of curiosity rather than harboring malicious intent or a desire for sabotage, highlighting the diverse motivations within the realm of hacking.

What You Will Find In this Hacking Book

This hacking guide offers a comprehensive exploration of the intriguing and intricate world of hacking. It delves into the evolution of hacking since the 1960s, examining its various applications over time. The guide aims to equip you with a solid understanding of hacking and its fundamentals, paving the way for you to engage in basic hacking activities. The motivations for hacking are diverse, and this guide acknowledges the legitimate reasons, such as securing personal information.

As you embark on the journey of learning hacking, the guide emphasizes that it is an attainable skill, dispelling the Hollywood myth that one needs exceptional technical genius. The book provides a roadmap and strategies tailored for beginners, ensuring that the presented techniques, while not the most sophisticated, are less risky than those employed by advanced hackers. It encourages gradual progress based on personal goals and work ethic, offering a beginner-friendly approach to hacking and facilitating the acquisition of information to become proficient in the field.

2

Introduction to Hacking

We've all encountered the media's portrayal of hackers, often depicted by Hollywood as intelligent individuals operating from their basements, effortlessly infiltrating any chosen network. While these portrayals are captivating, they fail to present the complete and accurate narrative of hacking. The term "hacker" originated in the 1960s, initially referring to programmers capable of crafting innovative computer code, essentially serving as pioneers who played a pivotal role in shaping the computer industry.

Initially, these early hackers were driven by passion and a desire to create and understand computer systems. They developed new programs and, if there were flaws in other systems, they contributed by creating patches to rectify issues. However, the dynamics shifted as computers transitioned into networks, expanding the hacker label to include individuals who gained access to restricted networks. Motivations for such access varied from curiosity to more malicious intentions.

The evolution of hacking over the decades has led to a distinction between historical and contemporary perceptions of hackers. The two sides of hacking, which will be explored further, operate differently, either exposing vulnerabilities or safeguarding networks.

Hacking, frequently featured in the news, is essentially the act of modifying computer software and hardware to achieve objectives beyond their original design. This broad definition encompasses unauthorized entry into networks. Those involved in hacking, known as hackers, may access computers and systems, seeking information for which they lack authorization.

Contrary to media portrayals, not all hackers engage in malicious activities. Some perceive hacking as a challenge or an exhilarating pursuit, while others simply enjoy exploring the capabilities of computers. The majority of contemporary hacking is not inherently destructive or criminal, although legal perspectives may vary.

Recognizing the skills of many hackers, some American corporations employ them on their technical teams. These individuals contribute to identifying security flaws and strengthening systems to prevent criminal hacking activities, ultimately enhancing cybersecurity measures.

Moreover, the impact of computer hacking extends beyond security considerations, contributing to technological advancements. Notable figures like Dennis Ritchie, a former hacker, played a crucial role in developing the UNIX operating system, influencing subsequent developments like Linux. Shawn

Fanning, the creator of Napster, is another example of a computer hacker who contributed to technological leadership.

Despite these positive contributions, the hacking world also harbors individuals with less noble intentions. Criminal hackers aim to steal personal information, infiltrate company databases, and gain unauthorized access to networks, leading to stricter laws, enhanced antivirus measures, and increased cybersecurity efforts.

In summary, the realm of hacking is multifaceted. While some hackers channel their interest in computers into constructive technological contributions, others pursue less honorable paths, seeking unauthorized access and information theft.

Common Terms to Know

Familiarizing yourself with essential terms is crucial now that you have an understanding of the hacking landscape. Acquainting yourself with these terms is vital for comprehending the content in the upcoming chapters. Here's an overview of some common terms in the hacking realm:

1. **Adware:** This software generates predetermined ads on your system. Some may be malicious, seizing control of your computer, slowing down the system, and hindering its use.

2. **Back door:** A point of entry into a computer or system that bypasses regular security, often utilized to access a computer

system or network. While developers may create it as a shortcut during development, forgetting to remove it can allow hackers access.

3. **Black hat:** The malicious hacker with intentions to exploit information for harmful purposes, potentially collaborating with other black hats to compromise systems.

4. **Cookies**: Information stored by a website in your computer browser regarding your search history, facilitating form completion. However, hackers can exploit this data if not periodically deleted.

5. **Cracker:** Hackers who illicitly infiltrate sites and networks, usually causing harm.

6. **Firewall:** A protective barrier on a system that prevents unauthorized intruders from accessing the network, whether in the form of software or a physical device.

7. **Gray hat**: An intermediary between white hat and black hat hackers, often exposing security flaws. While they may employ some illegal methods, they contribute to protecting individuals or companies.

8. **Key logger:** A program that records every keystroke on a computer, with the potential to compromise usernames, passwords, and sensitive information.

9. **Malware:** Malicious programs causing damage, including logic bombs, time bombs, worms, viruses, and Trojans.

10. **Phishing**: Deceptive messages, typically in emails, appearing legitimate but aiming to extract personal information from recipients.

11. **Virus:** Malicious code or program that attaches to files, replicating to infect other systems, similar to the flu's spread through networks, memory sticks, CDs, or emails.

12. **White hat**: Ethical hackers who employ their skills for constructive purposes, often hired by companies to maintain system integrity.

13. **Man in the middle attack:** Involves the hacker inserting themselves into a network to monitor and manipulate traffic and messages without detection by the sender or receiver.

14. **Brute force attack:** A time-consuming tactic utilizing all combinations of letters, numbers, and characters to gain access to a system when other alternatives fail.

15. **Denial of service attack**: A strategy to render a network or website unresponsive by overwhelming the server with an excessive volume of content requests.

16. **IP (Internet Protocol):** A unique address assigned to each device, serving as a fingerprint that allows hackers to locate, track activity, and identify users of the computer.

These terms provide a glimpse into the hacking world, showcasing various methods black hats employ to acquire information and gain control over computer systems. Understanding these terms and learning about hacking methodologies will deepen your comprehension of the diverse aspects of the hacking realm.

Common Myths Surrounding Hacking

Hacking, having been in existence for a considerable period, often carries misconceptions fueled by media portrayals. Exploring these misconceptions can lead to a clearer understanding of the hacking landscape.

1. Hacking is Always Illegal:

The prevalent belief that hacking is invariably illegal stems from media coverage focusing on malicious activities like unauthorized network access and the spread of malware. However, ethical hacking exists, involving individuals employed by companies to expose system flaws and enhance security rather than engaging in nefarious activities.

2. All Hackers are Young:

Another misconception suggests that hackers are predominantly young, often teenagers or in their early twenties. While some hackers fit this age profile, the truth is that hackers encompass individuals of any age who possess extensive computer knowledge and the ability to access restricted areas. Younger hackers may be more visible in illegal activities due to their relative inexperience.

3. Security Software Stops All Hacking:

The belief that robust security software ensures complete protection is flawed. While security measures can safeguard against certain threats, hackers often employ tactics to bypass these systems. User actions, such as clicking on deceptive links in emails, can compromise security, rendering software ineffective in preventing breaches.

4. Hacking Requires Specialized Software:

Contrary to Hollywood depictions, hacking does not necessarily demand specialized or illegally obtained software. Simple tools, like web applications, can identify vulnerabilities on websites. White hat hackers utilize these tools to enhance security, while black hat hackers exploit them for malicious purposes. Hacking primarily involves experimenting with various approaches until a system vulnerability is found, without the need for exotic software.

5. An Advanced Degree is Necessary to be a Hacker:

While some hackers may possess advanced degrees, particularly those working for major companies to identify system flaws, having an advanced degree is not a universal requirement. Many proficient hackers have never attended college, or at least not for computer-related studies. A passion for computers and the ability to learn the intricacies of their functioning are more crucial than formal education. Many hackers enter the field through self-learning at home, bypassing traditional college routes.

3

Ethical Hacking vs. Criminal Hacking

The realm of hacking consists of two distinct worlds. In one, individuals harness their hacking expertise to assist others altruistically. Whether in their leisure time or as part of their professional roles, they identify vulnerabilities or backdoors in corporate websites, notifying the concerned entities to fortify their security. Some of these ethical hackers are employed by hospitals, corporations, and various companies, dedicating themselves to locating and rectifying security weaknesses to ensure the safeguarding of personal information. Their hacking activities, though penetrating the system, are conducted ethically with the intention of providing assistance.

On the contrary, the other world within hacking is murkier, inhabited by individuals who employ their hacking skills for personal gain. These hackers exploit systems to access personal information, utilizing deceptive emails and links to solicit details for identity theft and other malicious purposes. Their actions are self-serving and lack any intention of aiding others.

Despite the shared use of similar tools in both worlds, the motivations behind hacking activities differ significantly. While the media predominantly focuses on black hat hacking, highlighting individuals facing consequences for their illicit actions, there exists an entire realm of ethical hacking that contributes positively to the world. This ethical hacking community plays a vital role in saving people substantial money, time, and headaches by proactively addressing and rectifying security vulnerabilities.

Ethical Hacking

Ethical hackers employ many of the same techniques as criminal hackers to breach network defenses, but their motives differ significantly. Their objective is to surpass security systems, identify loopholes, and offer guidance on resolving these issues. Many ethical hackers are employed by the corporations owning the targeted websites, creating documentation and devising plans to rectify identified vulnerabilities. Others, unaffiliated with the company, may discover loopholes and responsibly notify the relevant entities.

The essence of ethical hacking lies in assessing network security. Recognizing the potential threats posed by hackers seeking personal information, companies, especially those managing online stores and hospitals, engage white hat hackers to locate vulnerabilities. These professionals also analyze potential future malicious activities within the software. Vulnerabilities are often rooted in improper system configurations or software flaws, and white hat hackers work diligently to rectify them and safeguard valuable information.

Any company with an internet connection and a database containing clients' personal information should consider seeking assistance from a white hat or an individual with basic hacking knowledge. This approach enhances vulnerability management and customer protection.

While hacking has existed for some time, the concept of ethical hacking emerged in the 1970s when the U.S. government, aware of possessing substantial personal information, initiated the first ethical hacking processes. Experts, known as red teams, were brought in to hack into computer systems and identify vulnerabilities. This practice grew into a prominent industry within the information security market, with major corporations incorporating it into their infrastructure to enhance security.

Given the increasing exchange of personal information online, standards now mandate organizations connecting to the internet to undergo penetration tests. This test verifies the safety of information and addresses any existing vulnerabilities. Smaller organizations may occasionally hire ethical hackers for assistance, while larger companies maintain dedicated teams to continually fortify their defenses against intruders.

Ethical hackers play a crucial role in enhancing cybersecurity and have become a burgeoning field. Despite the lingering perception of hackers as mischief-makers or data thieves, ethical hackers utilize similar techniques to their black hat counterparts for benevolent purposes. This practice has gained popularity, allowing organizations to proactively manage their security. White hat hackers, working collaboratively with companies, navigate the hacking process to ensure the safety of clients' information from unscrupulous individuals. Some security professionals prefer alternative terms to "hacker" but operate in a similar capacity, aiming to assist rather than exploit.

Illicit Hacking

The flip side of hacking delves into darker territories. Instead of safeguarding others' personal information and ensuring a company's security, criminal hackers pilfer information for their personal gain. Infiltrating a company's network, they snatch emails and credit card details for their own use. Employing tactics such as spreading viruses, posing as someone else to solicit information, or initiating harmful activities, criminal hacking encompasses acts of intellectual property theft, identity theft, credit card fraud, vandalism, terrorism, and various computer-related crimes. Often violating privacy and causing damage to computer-based assets, criminal hacking frequently pursues financial gains for the perpetrator.

Numerous methods enable criminal hackers to access networks and exploit personal information maliciously. Viruses, Trojan horses disguising themselves as legitimate programs, and other surreptitious programs infiltrate computers to capture keystrokes and uncover usernames and passwords for email accounts, banking sites, and more.

One prevalent tactic employed by black hat hackers involves sending deceptive emails resembling legitimate sources, such as banks. Clicking on these emails can result in viruses or other computer issues. In more sophisticated schemes, hackers may send forms requesting personal information, deceiving individuals into providing details that are then utilized by the hacker.

The potential damage inflicted by black hat hackers is substantial, especially when individuals or companies fail to implement adequate computer safety measures. Financial losses, identity theft, and various other consequences may ensue, emphasizing the importance of vigilant monitoring for potential breaches.

Several infamous hacking incidents have occurred over the years, such as the case of David Smith, who unleashed the Melissa Virus in 1999. This virus affected 1.2 million computers, resulting in $80 million in losses for businesses in Europe and the United States. Smith, convicted of criminal hacking, initially faced a forty-year sentence but was released after less than two years in prison upon agreeing to collaborate with the FBI.

While not all criminal hacking incidents reach the scale of Smith's attack, they collectively incur millions of dollars in financial losses annually for businesses. The dynamic between black hat and white hat hackers unfolds as a race, with white hats striving to close vulnerabilities and backdoors on networks, while black hats attempt to exploit weaknesses or discover new avenues for chaos. Though white hats occasionally succeed in maintaining security, there are instances when black hats outpace them, inflicting damage on systems.

Both white hat and black hat hackers employ similar techniques to infiltrate computer systems, gaining access, inspecting information, and executing various tasks. The distinction lies in the ethical hacker's motivation to identify vulnerabilities and rectify them, while the criminal hacker is driven by a desire to acquire personal information, inflict losses on companies, and engage in malicious activities.

4

Passive and Active Attacks

There exists a multitude of potential incursions a hacker can execute on your computer, contingent upon the nature of the information sought from the network and the level of engagement they plan to invest in their endeavors. The various tactics employed by hackers can be broadly categorized into two groups: passive attacks and active attacks. Passive attacks are akin to investigative actions, where the hacker infiltrates the system but refrains from causing harm immediately, opting to explore the environment first. In contrast, active attacks involve a hacker who has acquired knowledge about the system and is prepared to initiate their disruptive actions. Let's delve into the distinctions between these two types of attacks and examine how hackers operate within each category.

Passive Attacks

Passive Attacks involve a strategy where the hacker patiently awaits the opportune moment to infiltrate a system and wreak havoc. The hacker gains access to the system and bides their time before initiating an attack. This approach allows the hacker to surreptitiously observe the target network, analyze the software in use, and evaluate existing security measures before launching their offensive.

Passive attacks primarily involve the hacker monitoring and identifying vulnerabilities within a system without making any alterations. It serves as a method for the hacker to clandestinely study the target system, enhancing the effectiveness of subsequent attacks. These passive attacks can be classified into two main types:

1. Active reconnaissance: By utilizing techniques like port scanning, the intruder listens to the targeted system, identifying potential weak points. This method proves effective in pinpointing vulnerabilities that can be exploited by the hacker.

2. Passive reconnaissance: In this approach, the hacker refrains from actively engaging with the system and instead focuses on studying it. Techniques such as masquerading, dumpster diving, and war driving fall under this category.

These tactics serve as valuable tools for hackers seeking to identify vulnerabilities within a computer system, enabling proactive measures to prevent future attacks. Employing reconnaissance strategies allows for the identification of weak points, and implementing security measures like Intrusion Prevention Systems (IPS) can further safeguard against automated methods, port scans, and other potential threats to the system.

Active Attacks

Active Attacks are designed to infiltrate a system and seize control of information, often causing more immediate harm as the hacker actively seeks unauthorized access and misappropriates data. The network might remain unaware of the hacker's presence, but the intruder can execute various actions to disrupt the system. Examples of common active attacks include:

1. Masquerade Attack:

In this scenario, the hacker impersonates a network user, deceiving the system into granting access to confidential files and information. The approach may involve backdoor methods, password/user ID exploitation, or security flaw manipulation. Once inside the system, the hacker gains privileges akin to a regular user, enabling actions like software alterations, file deletion, user expulsion, and more.

2. Session Replay Attack:

This attack aims to establish automatic authentication whenever the target accesses a specific website. By exploiting the web's storage of URLs, cookies, and forms in a browser, the hacker can perform session replay attacks, effectively operating on the system like any legitimate user. Since this attack doesn't occur in real-time, identifying it can be challenging for the legitimate user, often discovered when discrepancies appear in their account or after falling victim to identity theft.

3. Denial of Service (DoS) and Distributed Denial of Service (DDoS):

A DoS attack involves the hacker denying service or access to a legitimate user, causing services on the computer to slow down or stop working. Conversely, a DDoS attack entails a hacker compromising numerous systems to collectively target a specific victim. While these attacks may not aim to destroy a security system or steal data, they can result in profit loss or render the computer system unusable. Connectivity issues and service disruptions throughout the network may occur, potentially leading to file destruction, depending on the hacker's objectives.

Identifying such attacks is akin to recognizing a slow internet connection, manifesting as reduced network performance and restricted access to desired websites. Warning signs include an influx of spam or unusual traffic, prompting users to investigate potential hacking indicators.

5

Mapping Out Your Hacks

When embarking on the journey of hacking, it's crucial to devise a strategic plan. Every hacker must possess a clear understanding of their objectives and identify potential vulnerabilities in the targeted system. Before delving into the various strategies for successful hacking, let's explore the process of mapping out your hacking endeavors.

In the quest to discover vulnerabilities, there's no need to assess all security protocols on your devices simultaneously. Such an approach can lead to confusion and potentially create more problems than solutions due to the overwhelming volume of information. The key is to break down the testing process into manageable segments.

It is often prudent to initiate the assessment with a single system or application, gradually progressing through the list one step at a time. When deciding which system to prioritize, consider the following questions:

1. In the event of an attack, which system would pose the most significant challenges or be the most difficult to rectify if lost?
2. If subjected to an attack, which system is the most vulnerable and, consequently, the easiest target for hackers?
3. Which components of the system being assessed are least documented and rarely scrutinized? Are there any elements that remain unfamiliar?

Answering these questions will facilitate the selection of systems for examination and assist in establishing appropriate goals for the hacking process. Keeping detailed notes throughout the journey streamlines the process, ensuring accurate documentation and enabling the identification and resolution of any encountered issues.

Project Organization

When preparing to conduct your examinations, it's essential to focus on testing various devices, applications, and systems. The elements to include in your assessments are as follows:

1. Switches and routers
2. Workstations, laptops, and tablets connected to the system
3. Client and server operating systems
4. Database, application, and web servers
5. Firewalls
6. File, print, and email servers

The number of tests required will vary based on the scope of systems and devices that demand attention. For instance, in smaller networks, comprehensive testing can be efficiently executed without unnecessary time consumption. Fortunately, this process offers flexibility, allowing you to allocate your time wisely based on the priorities that seem most logical.

Optimal Timing for Hacking

Another crucial consideration for individuals embarking on hacking endeavors is determining the appropriate time to commence their activities. When establishing your objectives, it's essential to schedule these tests at times that will create minimal disruption for other users. For instance, avoid conducting tests during the early morning hours if that happens to be the peak business period. Engaging in testing during such times not only hampers the productivity of other employees but could exacerbate issues, potentially causing further delays.

To mitigate these challenges, identify a timeframe that minimizes disruption. Often, conducting tests after regular business hours proves to be the most effective approach, ensuring minimal interference and providing ample time to rectify any errors that may arise. Additionally, it is imperative to communicate clearly with everyone else on the system before commencing the tests, providing details about the testing schedule, expected duration, and other relevant information. This proactive communication helps in fostering a cooperative and informed environment during the testing phase.

Visibility Assessment

To pinpoint the system's vulnerabilities effectively, it's crucial to adopt the perspective of a malicious hacker. Being intimately familiar with the system might hinder your ability to identify potential weaknesses, making it imperative to view it through fresh eyes. Although you possess an in-depth understanding of the system, a criminal hacker lacks some of that knowledge but can offer a new angle of perception. To discern what a hacker might see, distinct from your own viewpoint, it's essential to determine the pathways the system follows when someone is on the network.

As a hacker, various options exist for gathering these pathways, and a recommended approach involves conducting an online search. If you're conducting tests for an organization, perform a search related to that specific entity. For personal system tests, initiate a search connected to your identity. Execute a probe to ascertain what others can perceive about your system, utilizing local port scanners, tools for assessing shared information, and more to identify potential vulnerabilities.

Upon completing this phase, further online searches can enhance your understanding. Invest time in exploring:

1. Contact details linking to individuals associated with your business, using background checks through ZabaSearch, ChoicePoint, and USSearch.
2. Recent press releases detailing organizational changes.
3. Historical information on mergers and acquisitions in-

volving the company.
4. SEC documents relevant to the organization.
5. Trademarks, patents, and associated intellectual property.
6. Incorporation filings, often accessible through the SEC.

While this process may be time-consuming, it provides valuable insights into what information about your company is easily accessible to others. A simple keyword search may not uncover all pertinent details, necessitating a more advanced search to ensure comprehensive results. Armed with an understanding of what information is readily available online, the next step involves mapping the network to identify potential vulnerabilities.

Network Mapping

Now, it's time to devise your plan for ethical hacking. Initially, it's crucial to understand what others already know about the system. If it's your personal computer, maintaining exclusive knowledge is paramount. However, in a work setting, where multiple users access the network, ensuring confidentiality becomes more complex. Despite the perceived anonymity online, each search leaves behind digital traces that could compromise security.

One effective method to assess who has access to your network is by utilizing Whois. Although primarily used to check domain name availability, it also provides insights into domain registration. If your domain appears on Whois, there's a higher likelihood that your contact details and email addresses are publicly accessible. Furthermore, Whois offers details about DNS servers associated with your domain and information on tech support from your service provider. Supplementing this with DNSstuf can yield additional data such as email hosting, host locations, and spam listings.

Exploring alternative platforms like Google Groups and forums is imperative to ensure data security. These platforms often harbor extensive information about your network, even if you haven't personally shared it. A simple search might reveal sensitive details like domain names, usernames, and IP addresses, posing significant security risks. Fortunately, if confidential information is discovered on such platforms, it's possible to have it removed. This typically requires appropriate credentials, such as working in the IT department of the affected company, to file a removal request with the support personnel.

Privacy policies play a vital role in informing website visitors about data collection and protection practices. While transparency is crucial, disclosing excessive information, especially security protocols or firewall details, could inadvertently aid malicious hackers. Thus, it's essential to exercise caution, especially when drafting privacy policies for new websites or updating existing ones. Regular reviews of privacy policies are necessary to ensure they don't inadvertently expose sensitive company information that could compromise security.

Initiating the System Scan

While investigating traces of your network online, you're gaining insights into potential areas where hackers might launch attacks. Look for any potential points where a hacker could exploit vulnerabilities, considering the following steps:

1. Review the information obtained from the Whois search, examining how IP addresses and hostnames are laid out. This site facilitates the verification of information, helping identify potential attack vectors.

2. Conduct a thorough scan of internal hosts to assess what a potential user might access. Recognize the possibility of attacks originating from within the organization, making it challenging to pinpoint internal threats.

3. Utilize the system's ping utility, employing a third-party tool like NewScan Tools or SuperScan for simultaneous pinging of multiple addresses. If unsure about the gateway IP address, www.whatismyip.com can assist in locating it.

4. Perform an external scan of the system by examining all open ports. Use tools like Nmap or SuperScan to assess what others can observe on the network, complemented by tools such as OMnipeek or Wireshark.

These scans offer valuable insights into what others might discover when scanning your IP addresses. Without robust security measures, hackers can replicate your process, uncover details about the services you run (e.g., email and web servers), understand authentication requirements for network sharing, and potentially gain remote access. While devising strategies to block such attempts, having a comprehensive understanding of what potential attackers can discern at this stage is crucial.

Identify the Weaknesses

Once you comprehend how a hacker could penetrate the security system, it becomes more straightforward to determine the potential targets for the computer. Employing various tools to handle these vulnerabilities is essential. It's crucial to remain vigilant for forthcoming vulnerabilities; the absence of these issues at the initial stages doesn't guarantee their absence in the future. Staying alert to the system's dynamics is instrumental in safeguarding personal or company information.

6

Basic Spoofing and Man in the Middle Attack Techniques

Irrespective of whether you are an ethical hacker or engaging in criminal hacking activities, there are numerous strategies available to infiltrate a system. Successful hackers require strong research skills and the patience to identify vulnerabilities in a system or network before making their move. Through dedication and effort, they can employ various methods to access the network and gather the desired information. Masquerading and spoofing techniques contribute to making this process more accessible.

Forgery

Forgery stands out as one of the primary and most effective tactics employed by hackers. It involves the hacker assuming the identity of another website, software, organization, or individual. The objective is to deceive the security protocols, gain entry to the network, and access confidential information beneficial to the hacker. There exist various spoofing techniques favored by hackers, including:

IP Spoofing

In this method, the hacker conceals or alters their IP address to deceive the network into thinking they are a legitimate user. The hacker may be situated in a different geographical location and mimic an IP address meeting the criteria set by the network administrator. Once infiltrated, the hacker gains control over the network, manipulates files, and executes more actions undetected. This tactic is successful due to its ability to identify a trusted IP address, allowing the hacker to modify headers further, providing full access to the network. The hacker can peruse personal data, manipulate files, and send harmful packets without leaving any traces.

DNS Spoofing

DNS spoofing tricks users attempting to access a legitimate site by redirecting them to a malicious website controlled by the hacker. The hacker may commandeer a genuine website or alter a few letters to deceive users. Unwary users, oblivious to the trickery, might input sensitive information, make payments, and more, all while the hacker covertly collects the data. For this technique to work, the hacker needs access to the same

LAN as the target, often necessitating the discovery of a weak password on a machine within the network.

Email Spoofing

Email spoofing proves handy when hackers aim to bypass email security. Email servers are generally adept at discerning legitimate emails from spam or potentially harmful content, diverting the latter away from inboxes. However, email spoofing enables hackers to circumvent these security measures, sending emails with malicious attachments that might otherwise be filtered out.

Phone Number Spoofing

Phone number spoofing involves the use of fabricated phone numbers or area codes to obscure the hacker's identity and location. This technique enables the hacker to access voicemail messages, send text messages using the spoofed number, or mislead the target about the call's origin. By adopting a number resembling a government office, the hacker may coax the target into divulging personal information.

These attacks pose a significant challenge for network administrators, as they are challenging to detect. Hackers can navigate the network effortlessly, leveraging security protocols and engaging with users. This enables them to conduct more man-in-the-middle attacks with ease, causing substantial damage.

Interception Assaults

Another category of attacks commonly employed by hackers, often following a spoofing attack, involves Man-in-the-Middle (MitM) attacks. Some hackers opt for passive observation, merely viewing data without further action, while others engage in active attacks to cause disruptions.

A Man-in-the-Middle attack occurs when a hacker executes an Address Resolution Protocol (ARP) spoofing. In this scenario, the hacker disseminates false ARP messages across the network they have taken control of. These deceptive messages enable hackers to link to the IP address of an authorized user on the server. Once successful, the hacker intercepts and receives all data that users transmit to the compromised IP address.

Essentially, the hacker appropriates an IP address, making it their own, allowing them to receive files, communications, and other information intended for the original user. This grants the hacker access to the network while intercepting all its traffic. The attack may manifest in several forms:

1. Session Hijacking:

The hacker exploits the false ARP to seize the user's session ID, retaining information about the traffic. This pilfered information can be utilized later to gain access to the user's account.

2. Denial of Service Attack:

ARP spoofing in this context links multiple IP addresses to the target, causing an overload of data by redirecting the expected data for other IP addresses to one device.

3. Man-in-the-Middle Attack:

The hacker, by pretending to be non-existent within the network, can modify and intercept messages exchanged between two or more users. Legitimate emails may be intercepted, altered maliciously, and then forwarded to the intended recipient, who unknowingly opens the tampered information.

To execute a Man-in-the-Middle attack or ARP spoofing, hackers often use tools such as Backtrack, similar to Kali Linux. The process involves several steps:

Step 1: Research

Hackers must gather necessary data by using tools like Wireshark, enabling them to observe wired or wireless network traffic as a starting point.

Step 2: Monitor Mode

Activate a wireless adapter in monitor mode to detect traffic, especially effective in hubbed networks with lower security compared to switched networks.

Step 3: CAM Table Manipulation

For switched networks, hackers may attempt to alter entries on the Content Addressable Memory (CAM) table, allowing them to capture traffic intended for other users. This requires an ARP spoofing attack.

Step 4: Utilize Backtrack

Invoke the Backtrack software, replacing the target client's MAC address with the hacker's MAC address. This is done using the command "arpspoof [client IP] [server IP]." The order of IP addresses is then reversed, signifying authorization.

Step 5: IP Forwarding

For Linux users, activating the "ip_forward" feature simplifies packet forwarding. The command "echo 1 >/proc/sys/net/ipv4/ip_forward" aids in forwarding packets between the client and server.

Step 6: Traffic Analysis with Dsniff

Leverage BackTrack tools to sniff out and analyze network traffic, enhancing visibility.

Step 7: Data and Credential Extraction

Wait for the client to log onto the legitimate server, allowing the hacker to extract usernames and passwords. These credentials can then be exploited to gain access to various systems and services used by administrators and users.

This intricate process places the hacker in a central position, granting them access to intercepted information, credentials, and the ability to manipulate the system at will.

7

Hacking Passwords

Targeting Passwords

Hackers prioritize obtaining passwords because of their perceived simplicity to acquire. While many believe that longer passwords offer better protection, hackers, utilizing previously mentioned tricks, can intercept usernames and passwords regardless of their length.

Confidential login details, particularly passwords, are regarded as security's weakest links, relying solely on secrecy. Once the secret is exposed, security is compromised. This vulnerability is evident in significant security breaches where a company's login credentials are leaked, providing hackers unauthorized access to systems and sensitive information. Occasionally, users unintentionally divulge their passwords, making the hacker's task even more accessible.

So, how do hackers breach passwords? Various methods include physical attacks, social engineering, and inference. Several tools are employed for password cracking, such as:

1. **Cain and Abel**: Effective for Windows RDP passwords and Cisco IOS hashes.
2. **Elcomsoft Distributed Password Recovery:** Retrieves PGP and Microsoft Office passwords, useful for cracking distributed passwords.
3. **Elcomsoft System Recovery:** Sets administrative credentials, resets password expirations, and resets Windows passwords.
4. **Ophcrack:** Uses rainbow tables to crack Windows passwords.
5. **Pandora:** Useful for cracking Novell Netware accounts, both online and offline.

While some tools necessitate physical access, once a hacker infiltrates the protected system, encrypted and password-protected files become accessible. When physical access is unattainable, hackers resort to alternative methods, including:

1. **Dictionary attacks:** Utilize dictionary words against password databases to identify weak passwords.
2. **Brute force attacks:** Attempt all combinations of numbers, special characters, and letters until the password is cracked.
3. **Rainbow attacks:** Efficient for cracking hashed pass-

words, though limited to passwords under 14 characters.
4. **Keystroke logging:** Involves placing a recording device on the target system to capture all keystrokes, sending information to the hacker.
5. **Searching for weak storages:** Explores local password storage in applications, often vulnerable to a hacker's search during physical access.
6. **Remote password retrieval:** Involves a spoofing attack, exploiting the SAM file, and retrieving information remotely.

Once hackers acquire these passwords, they gain access to networks, emails, financial accounts, and more. Recognizing passwords as a significant vulnerability, it becomes crucial to explore more secure ways to safeguard systems.

8

Hacking a Network Connection

Engaging in Network Exploits

Another avenue a hacker might explore is compromising a network connection. By doing so, the hacker can mask their identity, access larger bandwidths for extensive downloads, and easily engage in illicit activities within the network. Once inside, decrypting user traffic becomes a straightforward task for the hacker, potentially leading to unauthorized access and data capture. The vulnerabilities a Wi-Fi connection presents can cause significant trouble for the target.

Before attempting to test-hack an internet connection, it's crucial to recognize the diverse levels and types of security measures protecting wireless connections. The extent of security in place will influence the feasibility and complexity of a potential network attack. Various wireless protocols come into play, including:

1. WEP (Wired Equivalent Privacy):

Primarily designed for privacy in wired connections, WEP encryption is relatively easy to crack. Hackers can capture the initialized vector, making older devices and inadequately updated wireless connections more susceptible to attacks.

2. WPA or WPA1 (Wi-Fi Protected Access):

Introduced to address WEP's weaknesses, WPA utilizes the Temporal Key Integrity Protocol. While sharing similarities with WEP, it incorporates enhancements that increase its resistance to attacks, without requiring users to install new hardware.

3. WPA2-PSK (Wi-Fi Protected Access 2 - Pre-Shared Key):

Frequently used by small businesses, this protocol allows users to employ a pre-shared key (PSK). While more secure than WEP and WPA1 due to added protection, vulnerabilities still exist.

4.WPA2-AES (Wi-Fi Protected Access 2 - Advanced Encryption Standard):

This protocol utilizes the Advanced Encryption Standard for data encryption. Systems employing WPA2-AES often incorporate a RADIUS service, enhancing security. While still susceptible to hacking, it presents a more challenging target than its predecessors.

Penetrating a WEP Connection

Breaking into a WEP connection is among the more accessible hacking endeavors. If you find yourself utilizing this type of connection, it is advisable to conduct tests to ascertain whether your system is vulnerable and to explore potential adjustments. To initiate this process, a hacker requires several tools, including BackTrack, aircrack-ng, and a wireless adapter. Here's a step-by-step guide:

Load up aircrack-ng in BackTrack: Launch BackTrack and insert the wireless adapter to verify its functionality. Use the command "iwconfig" to identify recognized adapters. Subsequently, enable promiscuous mode for the wireless adapter by entering "airmon-ng start wlano." This will change the interface's name to "mon0," allowing you to view accessible connections with "airodump-ng mon0."

Capture your access point: Choose the target connection for capture by using the command:

airodump-ng —bssid [BSSID of target] -c [channel number] -w WEPcrack mon0.

This initiates the capture of packets from the specified access point, crucial for decoding passkeys. Be patient, as packet acquisition may take some time. For faster results, injecting ARP traffic can be considered.

Inject ARP traffic: Expedite packet acquisition by executing an ARP packet replay. With the MAC and BSSID addresses obtained in the previous step:

aireplay-ng -3 -b [BSSID] – [MAC address] mon0

This command captures ARPs through the target's access point, ensuring continuous acquisition of IVs.

Crack the WEPkey: Once a sufficient number of IVs are accumulated in the WEPcrack file, proceed to run aircrack-ng:

aircrack-ng [name of file]

Aircrack-ng will present the passkey in hexadecimal format. Apply this key to your remote access point, granting you access to the network for various purposes, such as free internet usage or potential control over a computer within the system.

The Malevolent Twin Exploit

The previously outlined procedures offer a means of gaining access to a wireless network, possibly without authorized permission. Some hackers might find this sufficient for acquiring free bandwidth without any associated costs. However, alternative and more potent network connection exploits exist, providing enhanced access to the network beyond just securing free internet. One such formidable exploit is recognized as the

HACKING A NETWORK CONNECTION

malevolent twin access point hack.

The malevolent twin hack entails creating an access point that mimics the user's regular connection but is inherently deceptive. To the target, it appears as their familiar access point, luring them into a false sense of security. Unbeknownst to the user, the malevolent access point redirects them to the hacker's pre-established access point, initiating a perilous man-in-the-middle attack.

For those venturing into the malevolent twin attack as novice hackers, foundational steps include:

1. Activate BackTrack and initiate the "airmon-ng" program to ensure proper functioning of the wireless card, confirmed through "bt > iwconfig."

2. Transition the wireless card into monitor mode with the command "bt > airmon-ng start wlan0."

3. Commence capturing wireless traffic using "bt > airodump-ng mon0." This step allows visibility of all access points within range, facilitating the identification of the target.

4. Wait for the target to connect, then copy the BSSID and MAC address for subsequent hacking attempts.

5. Construct an access point mirroring the credentials of the target:
    - Open a new terminal and input "bt > airbase-ng -a [BSSID] –essid ["SSID of target] -c [channel number] mon0."

- This command generates an access point that appears identical to the original, ensnaring the target.

6. De-authenticate the target from their current access point with the command "bt > aireplay-ng –deauth 0 -a [BSSID of target]."

7. Amplify the signal of the malevolent twin to surpass the strength of the original access point:
   - Utilize "iwconfig wlan0 txpower 27" to boost the signal.
   - This adds 500 milliwatts to the power, but if insufficient due to distance, consider proximity or obtaining a newer wireless card capable of up to 2000 milliwatts.

8. Exploit the malevolent twin:
   - Upon confirming the target and the network connection to the malevolent twin, take necessary steps to monitor system activities.
   - Depending on objectives, hackers may engage in man-in-the-middle attacks, traffic interception, introduction of new traffic, or information theft, often without the target's awareness.

Infiltrating a network connection opens avenues for diverse possibilities, with some hackers seeking free bandwidth for substantial downloads, while others aim to inflict mischief and damage. Regardless of motives, it is crucial to understand methods for safeguarding internet connections to protect personal information from potential hackers.

9

Popular Tools for Hacking

Regardless of whether you're an ethical hacker or engaged in malicious activities, there exists a plethora of powerful tools designed to safeguard personal systems, fortify larger networks, or exploit vulnerabilities. These tools, often crowd-sourced through online hacker forums and hubs, serve to simplify tasks and identify system weaknesses.

Ethical hackers, in particular, leverage various common tools to detect vulnerabilities, perform controlled hacks, and conduct tests. Some widely utilized hacking tools, applicable to both criminal and ethical hacking endeavors, include:

1. Ipscan or Angry IP Scanner

- This tool is instrumental in determining the IP address of a target computer, aiding hackers in tracking them. It explores network ports to identify gateways for easier access to the targeted system. Ipscan is not exclusive to criminal hackers, as system administrators and engineers also employ it to identify vulnerabilities in their personal systems. Its open-source nature and efficacy make it a preferred choice for novice hackers.

2. Kali Linux

- Introduced in 2015, Kali Linux has become a favorite toolkit for hackers due to its extensive features. It focuses on security and can be run through USB or CD without installation on the computer. Capable of working across various interfaces, Kali Linux facilitates tasks like Wi-Fi password cracking, creating spoof messages, and generating fake networks.

3. Cain and Abel

- Tailored to Microsoft operating systems, Cain and Abel serve both criminal and ethical hackers. It enables the recovery of passwords for wireless networks and user accounts, employing forcing methods to crack passwords. Some users leverage Cain and Abel for recording VoIP conversation sessions.

4. Burp Suite

- A valuable tool for identifying vulnerabilities in websites or networks, Burp Suite scrutinizes each cookie on a website. Criminal hackers may exploit it to pinpoint security gaps, enabling them to take advantage, while ethical hackers use it to analyze website functionality and enhance security.

5. Ettercap

- Efficient for launching man-in-the-middle attacks, Ettercap convinces two systems they are communicating directly while the hacker acts as a relay. This enables data manipulation or theft during transactions and eavesdropping on network conversations.

6. John the Ripper

- Employing brute force to crack passwords, John the Ripper stands out for its efficiency in recovering encrypted passwords. Although brute force tactics can be time-consuming, John the Ripper is highly effective, making it suitable for recovering passwords and gaining access to networks.

7. Metasploit

- Celebrated among hackers, Metasploit efficiently aids ethical hackers in identifying network security issues. It serves as a network planning tool for beginners to check authorized access and potential unauthorized network entry points.

8. Aircrack-ng and Wireshark

- Often used in conjunction, Aircrack-ng and Wireshark facilitate the hacking of user passwords, IDs, and Wi-Fi connections. Wireshark acts as a packet sniffer, identifying wireless connections, while Aircrack-ng captures information for network access.

These tools represent just a fraction of the available resources for both ethical and criminal hacking pursuits. Staying updated on industry developments through hacking blogs and forums is crucial, as new tools continuously emerge, offering enhanced capabilities for system vulnerability identification and protection. Failing to keep abreast of these advancements could leave even ethical hackers susceptible to exploitation by criminal counterparts.

10

How to Hack a Website

Websites are a common target for hackers, presenting an opportunity for them to infiltrate and compromise computer systems when users access what appears to be a legitimate site. Various attacks can be employed to take control of a website, one of which is the directory traversal attack.

In a directory traversal attack, hackers exploit the website's directory, which essentially functions as the storage location for the site's files. By gaining access to this directory, they can navigate through its files, including sensitive ones like confi, htaccess, and root files. To illustrate, if a text file named abcdefg.txt resides in a directory named John, the hacker would input the command "….abcdefg" to move to the specific location, with the four dots indicating a movement up by two folders.

This type of attack, an HTTP exploit, aims to acquire restricted files or view random files on the web server, such as SSL private keys and password files. Often, hackers seek access to the server's root directory, employing techniques like dot slash to achieve this. Addressing this vulnerability is crucial for enhancing the security of web servers.

Hackers can employ tools like the HTTrack website copier, a spider program, to identify publicly accessible files within a website directory. This tool, easy to use and free, mirrors a website, revealing all records and files it contains. Many websites house sensitive information, including source codes and application scripts, making it essential to watch for file types like .rar or .lzip, as well as pdf and .html files that may contain valuable data.

Another method hackers use to locate public files is through Google. Advanced queries can unveil sensitive information, webcams, server directories, and even credit card numbers stored in Google's cache from website searches. Specific queries like "site:hostname keywords" or "filetype: file-extension site:hostname" help pinpoint the desired information.

It is imperative to exercise caution when sharing information online, as inadequate website security may expose data to hackers. Understanding and using operators like those in Google queries is essential to safeguarding sensitive information from potential cyber threats.

Securing Your Directory

The responsibility lies with the website developer to safeguard the website against potential attacks. There are three effective countermeasures to address these issues:

1. Careful File Storage:

Ensure that private, confidential, or outdated records are not stored on the server. Limit the contents of the DocumentRoot or the htdocs folder to essential files necessary for the proper functioning of the website. It is crucial to verify that these files do not contain sensitive information.

2. Control Search Engine Access:

Prevent sensitive data from being stored in the cache of search engines like Google by configuring the robots.txt file. This action restricts the indexing of confidential information by these search engines.

3. Directory Access Configuration:

Configure the web server to permit public access only to specific directories. Implement minimum privileges to control public access, ensuring that only essential directories required for the site's proper functioning are accessible.

Additionally, consider using the Google Hack Honeypot as an option. This tool attracts malicious hackers, allowing you to observe their techniques and subsequently implement appropriate countermeasures to keep them at bay.

Hackers often target websites to obtain personal information from clients or to launch attacks on other users of the site. Understanding the methods employed by hackers and employing effective countermeasures is crucial for maintaining the security of your website and preventing unauthorized access to any stored personal information.

11

Conclusion

Thank you for your purchase of this book!

I trust that this book has provided you with a deeper understanding of hacking, revealing its nuanced nature beyond the conventional black and white hat portrayal. Hacking encompasses diverse realms, and despite the negative image often portrayed by the media, there are numerous constructive applications for this skill in various aspects of life, devoid of malicious intent.

Now, the next step is to implement the techniques and strategies you've acquired. Designed for beginners with a passion for computers but lacking previous hacking experience, these methods offer a practical starting point for your journey. While not exhaustive, they serve as a foundation for your exploration into the world of hacking.

For additional valuable information and resources, I encourage you to visit our Amazon Author page. There, you can discover a range of books covering topics such as Python Programming, SQL, JavaScript, and even TOR if that aligns with your interests. Happy learning!

Expressing gratitude and wishing you success in your hacking pursuits!

www.ingramcontent.com/pod-product-compliance
Lightning Source LLC
LaVergne TN
LVHW020438080526
838202LV00055B/5258